# MAYER SMITH

# Beneath the Gilded Sky

First edition

This book was professionally typeset on Reedsy.
Find out more at reedsy.com

# Contents

# One

## The Unseen Connection

The grand ballroom was alive with shimmering lights and the soft murmur of the city's elite. The air was thick with the fragrance of expensive perfume, mingling with the faint smell of freshly cut roses from the grand arrangements that dotted the room. Lila's heels clicked softly against the marble floor as she made her way through the crowd, the hem of her deep red gown swaying with each step, reflecting the glow of the crystal chandeliers above.

She had never felt more out of place. The polished faces of the city's wealthiest swirled around her like a storm of glittering jewels, their conversations a constant hum in the background. Every so often, someone would look her way, their gaze lingering just long enough for her to feel the weight of their judgment—whether kind or critical, she couldn't tell. But tonight, it didn't matter.

Tonight was about business, about making her father proud, about securing her place in this gilded world she never quite belonged to. As the only daughter of one of the city's most influential businessmen, she was expected to make an impression. But Lila felt more like an observer, trapped behind the veneer of a perfect smile and the delicate curve of her neck. Her gaze wandered across the room, lingering on the extravagant gowns, the glint of cufflinks, the clinking of champagne flutes.

And then, she saw him.

Theo.

At first, it was a glance—a passing sight amidst the sea of faces—but something about him made her stop. It wasn't just his height, his sharp jawline, or the way his black suit seemed to hold an air of understated power. It was the way he moved, like a shadow moving against the tide of light and laughter. His presence was magnetic, but not in the conventional way. It was as if he didn't belong in this room, as though he were an echo of something darker, something she couldn't quite grasp.

Their eyes met across the ballroom, and Lila's breath caught. The connection was instantaneous, but not in the way she had ever experienced before. This wasn't the flutter of attraction or the easy familiarity of someone she had known. No, this was something entirely different. It was a silent understanding, a pull between them that felt both electric and dangerous.

For a moment, she wondered if he had been staring at her for longer than she had realized. But before she could make sense of the thought, he was gone, slipping through the crowd with the quiet grace of a man who belonged to no one and nothing.

She stood frozen for a heartbeat, unsure of what had just happened.  Her pulse quickened, and she had the strange sensation that the room had grown smaller, the voices quieter, the air heavier. She didn't know what it was—whether it was his presence or the strange pull she felt toward him—but she couldn't shake the feeling that her life had just shifted in some inexplicable way.

"Lila, darling, you're looking stunning tonight."

The voice was smooth, coated with practiced charm.  Her mother, always the social butterfly, appeared by her side, her hand resting lightly on Lila's arm.

"Thank you, Mother," Lila said, forcing a smile.

Her mother didn't seem to notice the brief flicker of distraction in her daughter's eyes. Instead, she steered her toward a group of guests, who were already gathering around the latest gossip. Lila followed mechanically, her thoughts still lingering on the man who had disappeared as quickly as he had appeared.

But he wasn't gone. Not entirely. His presence still hung in the air, like the lingering scent of something forbidden, something that was at once a temptation and a warning.

The night stretched on, but Lila's mind refused to settle. She mingled, made polite conversation with the familiar faces, but she was no longer truly present. She could feel her attention drifting, slipping toward the corners of the room where shadows seemed to congregate. Where she had seen him last.

It was during a lull in the crowd that she saw him again, standing near one of the tall windows that overlooked the city below. The way the moonlight struck him, casting a silvery glow across his features, made him seem even more enigmatic. His eyes were fixed on something in the distance, distant and unreadable, but Lila couldn't look away.

She knew she should turn around, go back to the conversation she had been in, but the pull was irresistible. It was as if her feet moved of their own accord, drawing her closer to him.

By the time she realized what she was doing, she was standing just a few feet away, her breath catching in her throat. He hadn't noticed her approach, his attention still fixed on the view. The room was alive with noise, but in that small corner by the window, it was as if the world had faded away, leaving only the two of them.

And then he turned.

The look in his eyes was intense, piercing, as if he had been waiting for her all along. There was no smile, no greeting—just a gaze that seemed to see through her, into places she hadn't even known existed.

"Lila," he said, his voice low and smooth, like a whisper across a vast, dark expanse. "You're far from home."

His words sent a shiver down her spine. She had never met him before, but the way he said her name… it felt like he had known her forever. Like he had been waiting for her to appear.

"I—" She stopped herself, unsure of what she had intended to say. Her usual composure faltered under the weight of his gaze. She wasn't sure if she was being drawn in by his presence or repelled by it.

"Are you enjoying the party?" His question was simple, but there was an undercurrent of something deeper.

"It's…" She hesitated, searching for the right word. "Overwhelming, I suppose."

"Not your scene?" His lips curved slightly, but the smile didn't quite reach his eyes.

"No," she admitted, feeling a strange honesty flood her. "I don't really belong here."

The words hung between them, more truthful than she had meant to be. She wasn't sure why she had said them, but it felt right.

Theo studied her for a moment, his eyes narrowing ever so slightly. "And yet you're here," he said, his voice almost a challenge.

Lila could feel the weight of his words, the layers beneath them. She wanted to ask him why he was here, too—why someone like him would choose this world, or what drew him to her. But she didn't. Instead, she found herself asking a question that felt far more personal, far more dangerous.

"What do you want from me, Theo?"

His eyes flashed, and for a moment, she thought she saw a flicker of something—something darker, more elusive. But just as quickly, it was gone, replaced by that same unreadable calm.

"Nothing," he replied, and for a moment, Lila believed him. "Not yet, at least."

The words felt like a promise and a threat, hanging in the air like a breath held too long.

Before Lila could respond, a voice called her name from across the room. Her mother, searching for her.

Theo stepped back, his gaze lingering on her one final time before he turned and disappeared into the crowd.

But Lila couldn't shake the feeling that their paths had crossed for a reason, that this night had changed everything. She didn't know why he had looked at her the way he did, or why his words had settled so deeply inside her, but one thing was certain.

She couldn't let go of him.

Not yet.

Not ever.

# Two

# Secrets in the Shadows

The sound of the city below was a constant hum, like the steady pulse of a living, breathing thing. Lila stood at the window of her father's penthouse, her hand pressed lightly against the cool glass, staring out over the skyline that stretched endlessly into the distance. The city lights twinkled like stars scattered across the dark fabric of the night, but despite the beauty, Lila felt none of its magic tonight. Instead, her mind kept returning to the brief, electrifying encounter with Theo.

Her heart beat faster just at the thought of him. She had spent the entire evening trying to shake him from her mind, but his gaze—so intense, so enigmatic—had stayed with her, haunting her in the quiet moments. And that voice, that whisper-like tone, had woven itself into her thoughts like a melody she couldn't forget.

She shook her head, trying to push the thoughts away. She had more pressing matters to attend to, after all. The gala had been a success, and the business deals her father had lined up were promising, but there was something else—something she couldn't quite put her finger on—that had been eating at her since she left the event.

It wasn't just the pull she felt toward Theo. It was the feeling that there was something she hadn't seen, some layer of this city's glitzy facade that was just out of her reach. Something dark and unsettling, like a shadow waiting to swallow her whole.

With a sigh, Lila turned from the window and walked across the sleek marble floors, her footsteps soft against the polished surface. Her father's penthouse was a masterpiece of modern design—glass walls, angular furniture, and a view that took your breath away. But tonight, none of it could shake the feeling of unease that clung to her like a second skin.

She needed answers.

Lila retrieved her phone from the counter, her fingers hesitating over the screen. She had tried to find information about Theo, but the results were always the same: nothing. No social media presence, no public records, not even a whisper of him in the press. It was as if he didn't exist outside of the world they had shared at the gala. She felt a cold shiver of uncertainty creep down her spine.

Why was it so hard to find anything about him?

Her thoughts were interrupted by a sharp knock on the door. She turned quickly, startled, her pulse quickening. Who could be visiting at this hour? Her father was away on business, and the staff had all gone home for the night. She approached the door cautiously, a flutter of nervous anticipation rising in her chest.

When she opened it, she wasn't surprised to see the familiar face of Daniel, her father's most trusted associate. But what caught her off guard was the look on his face—tense, tight-lipped, as if he was carrying some burden too heavy to bear.

"Lila," Daniel said, his voice low and cautious. "We need to talk."

She stepped aside, allowing him into the foyer, her mind racing. Daniel had been a fixture in her life for as long as she could remember. He was sharp, always impeccably dressed, and never gave anything away. But tonight, there was something about him—something in the way his eyes darted around the room, as if he were looking over his shoulder—that set her on edge.

"What's going on?" Lila asked, her voice tinged with both curiosity and concern.

Daniel didn't immediately answer. Instead, he moved past her into the living room, his shoes tapping softly on the marble floor. He seemed to be gathering his thoughts, weighing his words. Lila followed, her pulse quickening with each step.

"Lila," he began again, finally meeting her gaze. "You've got to stop asking about him."

Lila blinked, taken aback. "About who?"

"Theo." Daniel's voice was firm, his words wrapped in an unspoken urgency. "I know you saw him at the gala. I know you're curious. But you don't want to get involved with him."

Her heart skipped a beat. "Why? Who is he? Why are you acting like this?"

Daniel's jaw clenched. He looked away, his eyes briefly flicking to the windows as if to make sure they were alone. The air between them thickened with the weight of his silence, and Lila felt a surge of frustration bubble up inside her.

"Just trust me," he said, his voice low and strained. "Theo isn't someone you want in your life, Lila. His name... it's not something you should be asking about."

"Why?" Lila demanded, stepping closer. Her mind was racing now, questions tumbling over one another. "What's going on, Daniel? Who is he?"

Daniel's eyes flicked to her face, and for a moment, Lila thought she saw something flicker in his expression—fear? Guilt? He exhaled sharply, as if steeling himself for something, then took a step closer to her.

"You don't know what you're getting into. You've always been sheltered, Lila," he said, his voice laced with an odd mixture of concern and something darker, something more secretive. "Theo's not just some man at a gala. He's... connected. To things you don't understand. Things your father's never told you about."

Lila's breath caught in her throat. The words were like a slap to her senses. "What things? What are you talking about?"

Before Daniel could respond, there was a soft buzz from Lila's phone on the counter. Both she and Daniel froze, their eyes turning toward it in the same instant. It was a text message, and the number wasn't familiar.

Lila's stomach tightened as she crossed the room, her fingers trembling slightly as she unlocked the screen. The message was short, cryptic, and chilling in its simplicity:

"Stay away from him. He's not what you think."

Lila's fingers hovered over the phone, her mind racing. Theo? Had he sent this? But why? What did he know about her?

"What is it?" Daniel asked, his voice sharp, like a warning.

Lila didn't answer at first. Instead, she turned the phone toward him, showing him the message. Daniel's face went pale as he took a step back, his eyes widening in something akin to panic.

"I told you," he said, his voice strained. "You don't know what you're dealing with. This isn't just about Theo. This is about things—people—that your father's been involved with for years. Things you don't want to understand."

Lila's heart was pounding in her chest, her pulse echoing in her ears. She had known that something was wrong. She had felt it the moment Theo's gaze had locked with hers. But now, the sense of danger felt real, palpable, like a hand tightening around her throat.

"I need to know what's going on," she said, her voice cold, determination hardening her resolve. "Tell me everything."

Daniel shook his head, his expression a mixture of guilt and fear. "I can't. It's not my place to—"

But before he could finish, there was a sharp knock at the door. Both of them froze, and a deep sense of foreboding crept into the room like a heavy fog.

Lila turned slowly toward the door. Her heart raced. Who else could be here at this hour? And why did it feel like something terrible was about to happen?

"I'm not going to let you get dragged into this," Daniel said quietly, his voice strained. "Not when it's too late."

As Lila reached for the door, she wondered if this was the moment when everything would change. Or if it already had.

# Three

# A Dance of Deception

The ballroom was quieter now, the night stretching on like a slow, steady rhythm. The laughter, the clinking of glasses, and the quiet hum of conversation had all melded into a background noise Lila barely noticed anymore. Her thoughts were too consumed by the memory of the message she had received earlier. "Stay away from him. He's not what you think."

She didn't want to believe it. Not yet. She had spent years living in a world of polished facades, her every move scrutinized by her father's ever-watchful eyes, and yet, for the first time, the weight of something unspoken hung heavily in the air. She couldn't let go of Theo, couldn't ignore the magnetic pull he had on her. But the deeper she dug, the more she realized that every answer seemed to lead to more questions—questions she wasn't sure she was ready to answer.

And yet, she couldn't pull herself away. Not now. Not when his shadow seemed to linger in every corner of her thoughts.

The night had drawn on, the guests now scattered throughout the grand hall, their faces masks of excitement and idle chatter. Lila felt like a stranger in the midst of it all. She was supposed to be mingling, enjoying the night, yet her mind kept drifting back to the man who had first caught her attention across the crowded ballroom.

And there he was again.

She spotted Theo near the far end of the room, standing by a long table where delicate hors d'oeuvres were being served. His posture was casual, yet there was an air about him that suggested he was anything but relaxed. His eyes moved across the room, scanning the crowd as though he were searching for something—or someone. His gaze shifted, and for a moment, their eyes locked. A flicker of something passed between them, something that was too intense to ignore.

Lila's pulse quickened, her breath catching in her throat. He knew. Somehow, he knew she was watching him.

She forced herself to look away, suddenly feeling like the walls were closing in on her. The heat of the room, the thick air, the overwhelming sound of laughter—it was all too much. She needed space, needed to breathe. Her legs moved almost on their own, carrying her toward the grand balcony that overlooked the city.

The moment she stepped outside, the cool night air hit her like a wave, sending a shiver down her spine. She leaned against the wrought-iron railing, the chill of the metal seeping through the fabric of her dress. The view below was breathtaking, the city sparkling like a constellation of lights, but even the beauty of it couldn't quiet the unsettling feeling in her chest. She needed answers.

"Are you trying to run away from me?"

The voice came from behind her, low and smooth, like the distant hum of a storm. Lila's breath caught in her throat as she turned slowly. Theo stood in the doorway, his figure bathed in the soft light spilling out from inside the ballroom. His presence filled the space, commanding attention, and for a moment, Lila forgot how to breathe.

"I—I wasn't running away," she said, her voice betraying her. "I just needed some air."

Theo stepped closer, his eyes locked onto hers with an intensity that made her heart skip a beat. "It's hard to believe you're running away when you're standing here, waiting for me."

Lila couldn't look away. The way he said it, the way he moved, there was an air of certainty in his words—like he knew exactly how she felt. And that scared her.

"I didn't know I was waiting for you," she replied, her voice barely above a whisper. She hated how fragile she sounded. Hated how the words came out as if they were already a confession.

Theo's lips quirked in a half-smile, the faintest glimmer of something dangerous lurking beneath his calm exterior. He took another step toward her, closing the space between them with a fluidity that sent a jolt through her body.

"You're always waiting for the things you don't even realize you want," he murmured, his voice wrapping around her like a warm, seductive wave. "You just don't know it yet."

The air between them was thick with something unsaid, something that both terrified and exhilarated Lila. His eyes never left hers, and in the dim light of the balcony, she could see the storm raging beneath the calm facade he wore. The man she had met at the gala was still there, the enigmatic stranger with a history she couldn't yet understand—but there was something more now, something even more unsettling.

Lila swallowed hard, her mind racing. She wasn't sure what she was supposed to feel, what she was supposed to do. Everything about Theo felt like a mystery, like a puzzle she wasn't sure she was ready to solve. And yet, she was already so deep into it.

"I don't understand you," she said, her voice trembling slightly. "You're not like anyone I've ever met. And I don't even know why I'm standing here, talking to you."

Theo chuckled softly, his gaze flicking down to her lips before returning to her eyes. "That's the beauty of it, Lila. You don't have to understand me. All you need to do is feel."

A shiver ran through her, his words sinking into her skin like a sharp, unexpected chill. Her breath quickened, her pulse rising, but she forced herself to stand her ground.

"What are you hiding, Theo?" she asked suddenly, the question slipping from her lips before she could stop it. The words hung in the air, heavy and dangerous, like a declaration.

Theo's expression darkened for a brief moment, and in that fleeting second, Lila saw something—something raw and unguarded—that made her wonder if she had touched on something she wasn't meant to.

"You don't want to know what I'm hiding," he said quietly, his voice now tinged with something darker. "But I'll tell you this, Lila—sometimes, the truth is more dangerous than the lies."

Lila's heart thudded in her chest, and she could feel the pull of his words, the danger in them, like a magnetic force drawing her deeper into his orbit. And despite the warning bells going off in her mind, she couldn't bring herself to pull away.

Theo took another step toward her, his presence overwhelming. He reached out, his fingers brushing against her cheek in a touch so light, so fleeting, that it almost felt like a dream. But it wasn't. It was real.

"I think you know that, don't you?" he whispered, his breath warm against her ear. "That you're already in too deep to walk away?"

Lila closed her eyes for a moment, her breath catching in her throat as the weight of his words settled over her like a shroud. She didn't know what he was asking of her, didn't know what he wanted from her. All she knew was that the more she tried to escape him, the more he became all she could think about.

When she opened her eyes again, Theo was already stepping back, his hands tucked into the pockets of his coat, his expression unreadable.

"Think about it, Lila," he said quietly, his voice now laced with a note of finality. "You're not as free as you think you are."

With that, he turned and walked back toward the door, his figure disappearing into the darkness of the ballroom.

Lila stood frozen, her body still humming with the echoes of his touch, his words. Her mind was spinning, caught between the desire to understand him and the fear of what she might uncover. But there was no turning back now. She had already taken the first step into his world, and the only way out was forward.

And as the door clicked shut behind him, Lila couldn't shake the feeling that this was just the beginning.

## Four

# The Gilded Cage

The city stretched beneath her like a sprawling, sleeping beast, its lights flickering with a quiet, mechanical rhythm. Lila stood in the penthouse once again, the vast windows offering an uninterrupted view of the skyline—a skyline that had never seemed so far away. Her eyes traced the lights below, but her thoughts were a thousand miles away, lost in the memory of last night. Theo's words, his touch, lingered in her mind like a haunting refrain.

She had not meant for it to happen, but every moment since their encounter had only deepened the pull between them. It was as if some invisible thread connected them—one that tightened with every glance, every word, until she could no longer ignore it.

But there was something more, something dangerous in the way

Theo existed in her world, something Lila couldn't shake. The warnings—both spoken and unspoken—came at her from every angle. Her father's cryptic silence. Daniel's hurried insistence that she stay away. Even the way the world around her felt like a carefully constructed facade, as if the very walls of this gilded life were closing in around her.

She stared at the reflection of herself in the glass, the woman she was supposed to be—polished, composed, and perfectly placed in a life her father had meticulously designed. Yet, deep down, she felt like an imposter. The more she got to know Theo, the more she realized how little she understood her own life.

The sound of a phone ringing broke her from her reverie. She turned sharply, her eyes darting toward the sleek surface of the coffee table where her phone sat. The name on the screen made her stomach tighten.

It was Daniel.

Lila hesitated for only a second before she answered, her voice steady, though her heart raced. "Daniel."

"You're not listening, Lila," came his voice, tight and controlled. There was a sense of urgency in his tone, something she couldn't quite place. "You need to stop—stop thinking about Theo."

"I can't," Lila said before she could stop herself. Her voice cracked, the truth spilling out before she could guard it. She bit her lip, cursing herself for the admission. "There's something about him, Daniel. Something I can't explain. I don't know what's real anymore."

There was a long pause on the other end of the line, and when Daniel spoke again, his voice was low, almost a whisper. "Lila, listen to me. This isn't just about Theo. There are things in motion, things that have been set into place for years. You don't know what you're dealing with. I can't protect you from it. No one can."

Her heart hammered in her chest, the weight of his words sinking deep. "I don't understand," she whispered, the sense of helplessness creeping into her voice. "What's happening?"

"You need to get out of this world, Lila. It's too late for you to stay in it and not be touched by it," Daniel said, his voice strained. "Theo… he's tangled up in things your father has worked his whole life to keep hidden. And if you keep pursuing him, you'll find yourself caught in something you can't escape. I'm not asking you, I'm telling you: walk away before it's too late."

The line went dead.

Lila stood frozen for several moments, the phone still pressed to her ear, her mind whirling. The fear in Daniel's voice, the cryptic warning—she had never heard him like this before. He was always composed, always in control, but now he sounded… desperate. And it was that desperation that made her chest tighten with dread.

What had he meant by "too late"?

Her thoughts were cut short by a soft knock on the door. Lila turned quickly, her pulse quickening once more. She wasn't expecting anyone. Not this late.

The knock came again, this time more insistent, and against her better judgment, she crossed the room to answer it.

When she opened the door, the man standing before her wasn't Daniel. It wasn't even anyone she recognized.

It was Theo.

He was dressed in a simple black coat, his dark eyes unreadable as they fixed on hers. A flash of something unspoken passed between them, a wave of recognition that hit Lila in the chest like a punch. She took a step back, not knowing whether she was inviting him in or instinctively retreating from him.

"Lila," Theo's voice was low, velvet-smooth, but there was a hint of urgency in it that made her heart race. "Can we talk?"

Her mind screamed at her to shut the door, to send him away, but her body moved on its own accord. She stepped aside, allowing him to enter.

The door clicked shut behind him, and for a long moment, neither of them spoke. Lila could feel the weight of his presence in the room, as if the air itself thickened around them. She turned to face him, her heart racing in her chest.

"What are you doing here?" she asked, trying to keep her voice steady. "How did you even find me?"

Theo's lips quirked in a faint smile, though there was something hard in his expression. "Does it really matter?" he asked, stepping closer to her. The air between them seemed to crackle with unspoken tension. "What matters is that I'm here now."

Lila opened her mouth to say something, but the words caught in her throat. She wanted to ask him all the things that had been weighing on her since the moment they met. Why he was so elusive, why he made her feel like she was standing on the edge of something vast and terrifying. But when he looked at her, when his gaze pierced through her like it always did, everything else fell away.

She had never felt more alive, more vulnerable, than she did in his presence.

"You shouldn't be here," she said quietly, her voice a mixture of defiance and something softer, something she didn't want to admit. "You're dangerous, Theo."

He didn't flinch at her words. In fact, there was a flicker of amusement in his eyes. "Dangerous? Maybe. But so are you, Lila." His words hung between them like a dare, like an invitation she wasn't sure she was ready to accept.

He reached out then, his hand brushing against hers. The touch was light, almost tentative, but it sent a jolt through her, like electricity arcing between them. Lila's breath caught in her throat, her body betraying her as she leaned into the touch.

"I don't want you to get hurt," Theo said, his voice rougher now, the edge of something dangerous creeping into his tone. "But I can't stay away from you, Lila. And I don't think you want me to."

His words were a challenge, a promise, a confession. And yet, Lila couldn't bring herself to pull away. She had never felt more conflicted in her life, her heart torn between the life she knew and the life Theo represented—a life of secrets, of danger, of things she wasn't sure she could comprehend.

"I'm already too far in," she whispered, her voice cracking.

Theo's eyes softened for a fraction of a second before the mask slid back into place. "Then you know what that means," he murmured. "There's no turning back now."

The words hung in the air like a trap, the meaning settling over her with the weight of inevitability. Lila wanted to argue, to step back, to run. But the part of her that had been drawn to Theo, the part of her that wanted answers, couldn't turn away.

The gilded cage that had once felt like home now seemed like a prison. And Theo? He wasn't the key to her escape. He was the reason she couldn't find her way out.

The door to the outside world slammed shut behind her as she took another step into his orbit, the darkness of the unknown swallowing her whole.

# Five

# Beneath the Surface

The city was quieter today. The hum of traffic, the chorus of voices, the constant rush—everything felt muffled as if a thick fog had descended on the streets. Lila stood by the window of her father's penthouse, her eyes tracing the faint outlines of the buildings in the distance, their sharp edges softened by the haze of a late afternoon fog. It should have been comforting, the stillness, the quiet that descended over the city as dusk began to fall. But for some reason, it only made her feel more unsettled.

The air in the penthouse was cool, but the silence in the room was suffocating. She hadn't seen Theo since the night he'd come to her door. His words still echoed in her mind: "There's no turning back now."

She didn't know what he meant by that—didn't know what it

would cost her to keep moving forward. But the deeper she got into this, the more she felt like she was being dragged under, like the surface was slipping away beneath her feet. And all the while, she couldn't escape the nagging feeling that something was wrong, that she was being led toward a precipice she wasn't sure she could survive.

Her phone buzzed on the sleek marble counter, the sound jolting her from her thoughts. For a moment, she considered ignoring it—everything seemed to blur together, everything felt like it could wait—but her fingers moved before her mind could stop them.

It was a message from Theo.

"Meet me. Tonight. I have something to show you."

Her pulse quickened, the familiar tension creeping back into her chest. He wasn't asking this time. He was telling her. And despite everything—despite the warnings, despite Daniel's cryptic words—she knew she couldn't say no.

She typed a quick reply, her fingers trembling slightly as she did. "Where?"

The response was immediate. "You'll know."

Lila set the phone down with a soft exhale, the weight of the decision pressing down on her like a thousand pounds. She should have stayed away. She knew that. But there was something about Theo—something dangerous, something magnetic—that kept her coming back. She had to know what he was hiding.

And tonight, he would finally show her.

The evening passed in a blur. Lila found herself unable to focus on anything, her mind too consumed with what was coming. She told herself it was just curiosity, that she wasn't really interested in Theo as much as she was in uncovering the truth. But deep down, she knew better. She was already in too deep. The questions, the confusion, the way he made her feel—it all swirled inside her, creating a tension she couldn't escape.

By the time the sun sank below the horizon, painting the sky with shades of red and orange, Lila knew it was time. She slipped into a simple black dress, the fabric soft against her skin, and stood before the mirror, staring at her reflection. She looked calm, collected, the image of the woman her father had raised. But she didn't feel that way. Not anymore.

There was a knock at the door.

Her heart leapt into her throat. She wasn't sure if it was anticipation or fear, but it didn't matter. Theo was here.

Lila opened the door slowly, and there he was. Theo, standing in the doorway, his dark eyes fixed on hers with that same intensity that sent a shiver down her spine. His expression was unreadable, his face as enigmatic as ever. He wasn't smiling, but there was something in the way he looked at her that made her feel both vulnerable and alive.

"Are you ready?" he asked, his voice low, almost a whisper.

Lila nodded, unable to find her voice. Instead, she stepped aside, allowing him to enter. The air between them felt thick, like a storm on the verge of breaking.

Theo didn't waste any time. He moved across the room quickly, his presence overwhelming. "We need to leave," he said. "It's not safe here."

Lila's brow furrowed. "Safe from what?"

"You'll understand soon enough." His eyes met hers, and for the briefest moment, something flickered in their depths. Fear? Regret? She couldn't tell. But it was gone before she could fully comprehend it.

Without another word, Theo led her out of the penthouse, the cool night air sweeping around them as they descended in the elevator. Lila's heart was pounding in her chest, her breath shallow as she tried to steady herself. She had no idea where they were going, only that something dangerous was coming, something that would change everything.

They drove in silence, the city blurring past them as the car hummed steadily along the road. Lila kept her gaze fixed on the window, watching the dark outlines of buildings pass in the night, but her mind was a whirlwind of thoughts. Every part of her wanted to ask Theo what was going on, wanted to demand answers, but something in his expression told her that now was not the time.

They pulled up to an old, seemingly abandoned building on the outskirts of the city. The windows were dark, the brick facade cracked and weathered, as if the place had been forgotten by time. Lila's gut twisted, a sense of dread settling in her bones. She didn't want to go in. Everything in her screamed to turn around, to walk away.

But she couldn't.

Theo stepped out of the car first, his long coat billowing behind him as he moved toward the door. Lila followed, her steps hesitant but determined. As they entered the building, the smell of dust and decay hit her, the air thick with the scent of old wood and rusted metal. The floors creaked beneath their feet, the sound echoing through the cavernous space.

"Where are we?" Lila's voice was barely a whisper, her eyes scanning the room. The place felt wrong, like something was waiting in the shadows.

Theo didn't answer right away. He led her down a narrow hallway, the walls lined with faded photographs and old portraits. The flickering of a single lightbulb overhead made the shadows dance across the walls, creating strange, fleeting shapes.

"I need you to understand," he said finally, his voice low and serious. "Everything I've told you, everything you've learned so far—it's all connected. You're deeper in this than you think, Lila."

She stopped in her tracks. "What do you mean? What do you

mean by this?"

Theo turned to face her, his expression hardening. "I'm trying to protect you. But you're not going to like the truth."

Lila's pulse quickened, her anxiety rising. She wanted to turn back, to leave the building and never look back. But the part of her that had come here, the part of her that had followed Theo, was still there. She couldn't let go now.

Theo reached out and took her hand, his fingers cold against hers. For a brief moment, Lila thought she felt the faintest tremor in his grip, but it was gone before she could be sure.

"Come," he said softly. "It's time you saw everything."

He led her deeper into the building, down a set of stairs that led to a dimly lit basement. The air was thick with the smell of earth and dampness, and the walls were lined with shelves of old, dusty books. But it wasn't the books that caught her attention.

It was the safe.

Standing in the center of the room, the massive, iron door was ajar, revealing the secrets hidden inside. Papers, photographs, files—everything she needed to know, everything that had been hidden from her, lay within that room.

Theo stepped aside, his eyes never leaving her face. "This is where the answers are."

Lila stood frozen at the door, her breath catching in her throat. The truth—everything she had been searching for—was within reach. But so was the danger. And as she took a step into the room, she couldn't shake the feeling that there was no turning back.

Not anymore.

# Six

# The Heart's Dilemma

The air was thick with a charged stillness, the kind that settled over a room just before a storm. Lila's fingers trembled as she ran them over the edge of the old, leather-bound books that lined the shelves of the dimly lit room. The musty scent of aged paper and dust clung to the air, thickening the atmosphere as if time itself had forgotten this place. It was silent, save for the low hum of Theo's breathing behind her, the only sound that made her painfully aware of his proximity.

Her heart hammered in her chest, not from the overwhelming presence of the documents in front of her, but from Theo's steady, magnetic pull. She had crossed into a world of secrets, and each step deeper felt like she was walking on a tightrope with no safety net beneath her.

The safe—the one she'd been drawn to—was open now, the contents spilling out in stark contrast to the cold stone walls surrounding them. Photographs, papers, and files were scattered across the floor as though someone had been rifling through them in a frantic search. Each image, each page, carried the weight of a history she couldn't yet understand. A history that was now entwined with hers in ways she couldn't escape.

She felt his presence behind her, his energy pressing against her like a wall. Theo didn't speak; he didn't need to. His silence was louder than anything he could have said, a quiet declaration that whatever lay ahead was theirs to face together—or perhaps it was only for her to face alone.

The truth was unraveling at a pace she could no longer control.

"You should see this," she said, her voice strained, her eyes focused on a photograph she had picked up from the floor. It was an old picture, black and white, of a man Lila didn't recognize, standing in front of what looked like a government building. But there was something about the man's face—something oddly familiar about the eyes staring back at her—that made her stomach turn.

Theo didn't reply immediately. She could feel him watching her, the weight of his gaze burning into her skin, but she didn't dare look up. If she looked at him, she might never be able to pull herself away. The feeling in her chest was suffocating, but it wasn't just the danger. It was the desire, the need to understand everything he had so carefully hidden from her. She couldn't let go of that pull, no matter how dangerous it became.

He stepped forward then, his footsteps quiet but deliberate. "That man is the key to all of it," Theo said, his voice thick with an intensity that made Lila's skin crawl.

The words sent a jolt through her, her grip tightening on the photograph as she finally turned to face him. "Who is he?"

Theo's eyes flickered to the image in her hand, but he didn't reach for it. Instead, he leaned against the wall, folding his arms across his chest. "He was a part of your father's past," Theo said quietly, as though testing the weight of his own words. "A past that, until now, you've never been allowed to see. Not until it was too late."

Lila's stomach twisted, the weight of those words sinking deep into her chest. Her father's past? What could be so horrible, so dangerous, that he would go to such lengths to keep it from her? She had always known that her father was a man of secrets, but this felt different. This felt like the unraveling of everything she had thought she knew about the world—and about her own life.

She set the photograph down, her fingers brushing the edges of the other documents on the floor, as though looking for something, anything, that would make sense of it all. Her hands were shaking now, the cold, damp air of the basement pressing against her skin as she gathered a few of the papers, reading the small print that seemed to scream at her from the page.

"Your father was involved in something much bigger than you realize," Theo continued, his voice low and calm, yet laced with something darker, something more dangerous. "He's a part of a syndicate—a network of people who have been pulling strings in this city for years. Your father was at the center of it."

Lila could barely breathe as the pieces of the puzzle began to fall into place, but even then, it didn't make sense. The man who had raised her, the one who had built an empire, who had kept their family at the very pinnacle of society—he was involved in something so dark? It didn't seem possible.

"No," she whispered, more to herself than to Theo. "That can't be true. My father… he would never."

Theo's gaze hardened, his jaw tightening as he approached her, his voice now barely above a whisper. "You don't know him the way I do. You don't know what he's capable of."

Her breath caught in her throat, and for a moment, she almost felt like she was drowning. There were too many questions, too many truths she wasn't ready to hear. And yet, a small, dark part of her knew that this was only the beginning. There was no turning back now.

She wanted to shout at Theo, to demand answers, to scream at him for pulling her into this mess. But the words didn't come. Instead, she stood there, staring at him, her pulse quickening as the walls of the room seemed to close in around her.

Theo seemed to sense her inner turmoil, his expression softening slightly, though the tension in his eyes remained. "I'm not here to hurt you, Lila," he said, his voice almost gentle now. "I never wanted you to get caught up in this. But I can't protect you from the truth. It's already too late."

The words hit her like a punch to the gut. Too late. That was all it had been. From the moment she had met him, from the moment they had crossed paths at the gala, everything had changed. There was no undoing it now. The web had been spun, and she was already caught in its threads.

She stepped away from him, moving toward the shelves, her fingers brushing against the rows of books in a futile attempt to ground herself. But everything felt so distant now, so foreign. The life she had known, the world she had been raised in—it was crumbling beneath her, and she had no idea what would rise from the ashes.

Theo's voice broke the silence. "You need to understand, Lila," he said, his words a whisper, a command. "This isn't just about your father. It's about you. You're involved now, whether you like it or not. And the longer you wait, the harder it will be to get out."

Her chest tightened as his words sunk in. She had always thought of herself as someone who could navigate the complex world she lived in—someone who could play the game, understand the rules. But now, as she stood there, surrounded by the remnants of a past she could no longer ignore, she realized just how powerless she was.

"Why me?" she whispered, her voice cracking with the weight of it all. "Why did you have to drag me into this?"

Theo took a step toward her, his expression unreadable as he reached out to touch her arm. The contact was brief, but it sent a shock of electricity through her, making her heart race.

"Because you're the key," he said simply. "And I need you to understand what's at stake. Not just for me, but for everyone you care about."

Lila's pulse quickened, her mind racing. She wanted to pull away, to shut herself off from him, from this reality that was spiraling out of control. But there was something in his eyes, something in the depth of his gaze that made her hesitate.

In the midst of the chaos, the tension, the overwhelming sense of danger that hung in the air like a storm cloud, one thing remained clear. Her heart—despite everything—was still caught in the web of Theo. And for better or worse, she couldn't find the strength to pull away.

"Tell me everything," she said, her voice barely above a whisper, the weight of her decision settling on her like a final sentence.

Theo's eyes darkened, but there was something almost... relieved in his gaze.

"I will. But you need to be ready."

The storm was closing in, and there was no escaping it now.

# Seven

## Into the Abyss

T he city had never looked so alien, so cold. Lila stood on the edge of the balcony, the city sprawling beneath her like a labyrinth of steel and stone. The lights twinkled in the distance, but the glow felt hollow now, as though the beauty of it all was a mere illusion hiding the rot beneath. The wind tugged at the edges of her dress, sending a shiver down her spine as she tried to steady her thoughts.

Theo had left her with too many questions and revelations, and now the answers seemed further out of reach than ever. They had spent hours pouring over the contents of that hidden room—the files, the photographs, the dark and tangled history that had once belonged to her father—and now to her. The weight of it all was unbearable, pressing down on her chest as though the very air in the room had thickened, suffocated by the secrets that lay bare before her.

She should have been terrified, should have run as far away from this madness as she could. But there was something in her—something she couldn't name—that made her stay. The truth, no matter how twisted, had a hold on her now. She couldn't simply walk away.

The low sound of footsteps broke through her thoughts, and her heart skipped a beat. Without turning around, she knew who it was.

"Are you going to stand there all night?" Theo's voice came from behind her, low and steady. He didn't sound angry, or even frustrated. His tone was… resigned, as though he, too, had given up on the possibility of escape.

Lila didn't answer him at first, instead staring down at the city below. "I don't know what I'm doing, Theo," she whispered, more to herself than to him. "I never wanted to be a part of this. I never asked for this… this life."

She felt him move closer, the soft click of his boots on the stone floor of the balcony growing louder as he approached. She didn't flinch when he stopped just behind her, his presence overwhelming, but comforting in its own way.

"I know," he murmured. "I never wanted you to get dragged into it either. But now that you're here, I can't protect you from it anymore."

Lila turned her head just enough to see him, her gaze meeting his for the first time since they had stepped into the forgotten room beneath her father's penthouse. His face was unreadable, but the weight of what he said hung between them like a thick fog.

"I don't want you to protect me," she replied softly. "I want the truth. All of it."

Theo's eyes darkened at her words. For a moment, he was silent, as if contemplating how much of the truth he could actually give her. He reached out, his fingers brushing lightly against her arm, sending a ripple of warmth through her, despite the chill in the air. The contact, so brief, yet so intimate, unsettled her more than the words ever could.

"You're right," he said quietly. "You deserve to know everything."

The wind shifted, the hairs on the back of her neck standing on end as the world around her seemed to shrink. This was the moment. The moment when she would either walk away, or cross the line she could never return from.

Lila took a deep breath, her heart hammering in her chest. "What did my father do, Theo? What was he involved in?"

Theo's jaw tightened, his gaze flickering toward the city, as if he, too, were trying to gather the courage to say what needed to be said. "Your father was part of something much bigger than you realize. He was involved in a network of power and control that spanned far beyond the city. But it wasn't just about business or politics. It was about influence—manipulation, using people to achieve an agenda."

Lila's stomach churned as she processed his words. "And you? Where do you fit into all of this?"

Theo exhaled slowly, and for a moment, she thought he might refuse to answer. But then his eyes met hers, and the coldness that had once been there seemed to thaw.

"I wasn't supposed to get involved either," he said, his voice rougher now. "I was supposed to stay away. But your father— he made sure that wasn't an option. He needed someone to watch over things. To make sure that certain… decisions were made. I was the one who made sure they didn't get out of hand. But then I met you. And everything changed."

Lila felt a surge of emotion—anger, confusion, fear—wash over her. She turned her body to face him fully, her hands trembling as she clasped them in front of her. "You knew all along, didn't you?" she asked, her voice sharp. "You knew who I was, who my father was, and you still let me walk into all of this. You let me trust you."

Theo didn't flinch at her words. Instead, his gaze softened, a flicker of guilt crossing his features, though it was quickly masked. "I didn't want to drag you into this, Lila. I didn't want you to become a part of it. But I didn't have a choice. You were already in danger. The moment I saw you, I knew I couldn't keep you away from it. I didn't want to, but I couldn't stop it."

Lila's breath caught in her throat, the depth of his words settling over her like a weight. "You don't get to make decisions for me," she whispered, though her voice wavered. She wanted to scream at him, to demand he explain how much of her life had been manipulated, how much of her future had already been written by others. But even as the words formed in her throat, a deeper part of her—the part that had always been drawn to him—understood. He had never wanted this for her. He had never wanted to be the one to drag her into the darkness.

"I didn't want to hurt you," he said, his voice soft, almost pleading. "But you need to understand, Lila, you're already part of this. It's too late to go back now."

Her heart ached at the look in his eyes, at the vulnerability that flickered there. She wanted to hate him. She wanted to push him away and scream that this wasn't her life, that she wasn't a pawn in some twisted game. But the truth was, she felt just as caught as he was—trapped in a web of fate, manipulated by forces that neither of them fully understood.

Lila's breath hitched as she took a step toward him. "What happens now?" she asked, her voice barely above a whisper.

Theo didn't immediately answer. Instead, he stepped closer, closing the distance between them, his hand reaching out to gently cup her cheek. The warmth of his touch sent a jolt through her, and for a moment, everything else faded away— the city, the danger, the lies. All that existed was the tension between them, thick and undeniable.

"You need to trust me," he said, his voice low and filled with a quiet desperation. "I'll protect you, Lila. I won't let anything happen to you."

She wanted to say something—to pull away, to demand that he explain everything, to make him promise her that she wouldn't lose herself in this—this abyss they were both falling into. But instead, she closed her eyes, leaning into his touch, feeling the thrum of his pulse against her fingertips as they brushed lightly across his chest.

In that moment, she didn't know if she was falling in love with him—or if she was simply falling.

But she knew one thing for sure.

There was no going back now. The abyss was pulling them both in, and they were both too far gone to escape.

# Eight

# The Burning Bridge

The sound of the rain came like a whisper at first, gentle against the windows, but as the storm grew stronger, it became a relentless pounding—a chorus of nature's fury that rattled the glass. Lila stared out at the darkened city, her hands pressed against the cool, rain-speckled window. The world outside felt impossibly distant, as if the city had become an unreachable landscape that no longer held any meaning. Everything was shifting. Everything was breaking apart, and she couldn't stop it.

She had always prided herself on her ability to stay grounded, to keep her composure no matter the storm. But that was before Theo. Before the lies and the secrets, before the cold reality that her father's empire was built on blood and manipulation. She had thought she knew who she was, but now, every truth she had held dear seemed like it was crumbling away, like the very foundations of her life were giving way beneath her feet.

The soft click of the door opening broke her from her thoughts. Lila didn't have to turn around to know who it was. Theo's presence had become an undeniable part of her life, an imprint on her soul that she couldn't erase.

Without a word, he crossed the room, his footsteps quiet on the marble floor, the heavy scent of rain following him like a shadow. When he stood beside her, close enough that she could feel the heat of his body, she turned, her eyes meeting his. His face was drawn, his usually confident posture now stiff and tense.

"Lila," he said, his voice low, gravelly, almost as if he had been carrying a weight for far too long. There was no smile, no warmth in his eyes. Just the harsh edge of someone who had seen too much, had done too much.

She opened her mouth to speak, but the words caught in her throat. There were too many things to say—too many questions that she wasn't sure she wanted to hear the answers to. Her hands clenched into fists at her sides, the storm outside somehow matching the turmoil inside her.

"Why did you do it?" Her voice was barely above a whisper, but it cut through the tension like a knife.

Theo didn't flinch. Instead, he stood there for a long moment, his eyes dark and unreadable. "I didn't want to. But I had no choice," he said, his words hanging heavy between them. He ran a hand through his hair, the motion so tired, so resigned, that it made something inside her break. "This wasn't supposed to happen, Lila. You weren't supposed to get involved. But you're already in the middle of it, and I—" He broke off, as if searching for the right words. But there were none.

Lila's chest tightened, a wave of confusion and anger bubbling up from deep inside her. "What exactly am I in the middle of, Theo? What is this? What am I supposed to believe?"

"You've seen it," he said quietly, his voice rougher now, as if the truth had been weighing on him too. "You've seen the files. The history. Your father's involvement with everything—everything that's been built on lies and deceit. The syndicate. The network." His eyes flickered to hers, and for a moment, something in his gaze softened, almost as if he was pleading with her to understand. "I never wanted you to know about any of it. I never wanted you to be a part of this. But now—"

"Now it's too late," she finished for him, the bitterness in her voice almost making her own stomach turn. The words felt like fire on her tongue, and yet they didn't carry the satisfaction she had hoped for. She had thought that confronting him would bring some sort of relief, some sort of closure. But it didn't. It only made her feel more lost, more tangled in this mess than ever before.

Theo took a step forward, closing the gap between them, his hand reaching out to gently touch her arm. The contact sent a shock of warmth through her, the heat of his touch searing through the fabric of her dress. She stiffened, instinctively stepping back, but his hand didn't let go. He held her gently, the grip firm but not demanding. His eyes searched hers with a depth of emotion that made her pulse race.

"I didn't want this for you," he said, his voice barely a whisper, the words filled with an aching sincerity. "I didn't want to bring you into this world, Lila. But now I can't let you go. I can't let you walk away from it."

She swallowed hard, trying to steady the whirlwind of emotions swirling inside her. His words felt like a threat, like a declaration of ownership, but there was something in the way he looked at her that made her heart tremble. His touch. His intensity. It wasn't just the danger that made him impossible to ignore. It was the way he made her feel—alive, and yet more vulnerable than she had ever been.

"You don't get to make that choice for me," she said, her voice shaking slightly, though she tried to keep the edge of defiance. "You don't get to decide for me what happens next."

Theo's eyes hardened for a moment, his jaw clenched, but then the softness returned, that vulnerability that he had tried so hard to conceal. "I'm not trying to control you, Lila. I'm trying to protect you. From everything that's coming."

She shook her head, stepping back again, this time pulling away from him. "I don't need protecting, Theo. I don't need anyone to decide what's best for me." Her voice was firm now, as if saying the words out loud could make them real. But even as she spoke, the truth was there, gnawing at her insides. She wasn't ready to face the truth. She wasn't ready to confront everything that had been hidden from her.

Theo watched her for a moment, and for a brief second, Lila thought he was going to argue, to press her harder. But instead, he let out a slow breath, his shoulders slumping as if the weight of the world had just settled even heavier on them.

"Then walk away," he said quietly, almost as if he were conceding defeat. "Walk away from me. From all of this." His gaze never left hers, but there was something so final in his words that it made her chest ache.

For a long moment, neither of them spoke. The rain pounded relentlessly against the windows, the sound filling the silence between them, growing louder as if echoing the growing tension in the room.

Lila opened her mouth to say something, but the words caught in her throat. What could she say? What could she possibly say that would make any of this right? There was no right answer. No escape. Not anymore.

With a single, agonizing movement, she turned away from him, her back now facing the window, the city a blur of lights in the distance. "I don't know what to do anymore, Theo. I don't know who I am anymore."

Theo didn't answer. She could feel the weight of his stare burning into her back, and for a brief second, she imagined she could feel the pulse of his heart—like an echo of her own.

And then, without a word, he stepped back. The space between them felt like a chasm, a gaping void that seemed to swallow up any hope they might have had. The storm outside seemed to mimic the storm inside her. The world was tearing apart, and there was no way out.

"You'll figure it out," Theo said, his voice steady but strained. "I believe in you."

And with that, he turned and left, his footsteps echoing down the hall as the door clicked softly behind him.

Lila stood in the silence, the air thick with the weight of the words they hadn't said. The door closed, and with it, a chapter of her life was sealed shut. The bridge had burned.

And there was no going back.

# Nine

## Reckoning

The city seemed to breathe in the quiet hours before dawn. The streets, empty and slick with the remnants of the storm, reflected the pale light of the streetlamps like pools of liquid silver. Lila sat in the dimly lit living room of her father's penthouse, the windows thrown open to the cool night air, but she barely noticed the breeze that fluttered the edges of the curtains. Her thoughts were a whirlpool, sucking her deeper into a darkness she couldn't escape.

Everything had changed.  Her world—what she had known, what she had believed—had shifted beneath her feet, leaving her stranded in the middle of something far more dangerous than she had ever imagined. Theo, her father, the syndicate, the web of lies and secrets—everything was tangled together, and she could no longer untangle it without risking her life.

She ran her fingers over the edge of the coffee table, her mind racing as she tried to make sense of it all. She had seen too much. She had learned too much. The pictures, the documents, the whispered conversations she had overheard in the quiet corners of rooms. She could no longer ignore the truth: her father's empire was built on blood and manipulation, and she was a part of it.

The sound of footsteps, soft yet deliberate, echoed down the hall. Lila's heart skipped a beat, and her breath caught in her throat. She didn't have to turn to know who it was. Theo.

She had hoped he would stay away. Hoped that after everything, after the way she had pushed him away, he would finally leave her to pick up the pieces of the life she had once known. But deep down, she knew better. There was no escaping him now. No escaping the pull that had bound them together from the very first moment their eyes had met.

The door creaked open, and Theo stepped into the room, his presence filling the space with an intensity that was almost tangible. His gaze locked onto hers, the weight of his eyes anchoring her to the spot. He hadn't changed—still the same man who had walked into her life and shattered everything, but now there was something different in his expression. Something raw, something that made her heart ache with the uncertainty of it all.

She stayed seated, unwilling to give him the satisfaction of seeing her stand. She had learned to stand her ground, to maintain control, but it was getting harder every time he entered her world. Every time he spoke, every time his voice brushed against her skin, she felt that pull, that heat between them, and it terrified her.

"Lila," he said, his voice low, almost hesitant. "We need to talk."

The words felt like a dagger in her chest, a reminder of everything she had been trying to avoid. She couldn't escape it. She couldn't escape him.

"I don't think there's anything left to say," she replied, her voice steady despite the war raging inside her. She wasn't sure if she was trying to convince him—or herself. "You've made your choice. And so have I."

Theo took a step toward her, and her breath caught in her throat as the space between them shrank. There was something in his eyes, something that she couldn't name, but it made her heart beat faster. His hands, as always, were at his sides, clenched into fists, and she could see the strain in his posture, the way his jaw tightened as if he were holding back something far more dangerous than just words.

"I didn't want you to be a part of this, Lila," he said, his voice barely above a whisper, as if the words had been trapped in him for far too long. "But it's too late. You're already in it, and I can't protect you from the truth anymore."

The truth. The word hung between them like a dead weight. She wanted to scream at him, to ask him why he hadn't told her sooner, why he hadn't spared her the pain of learning it all the hard way. But she couldn't. The words caught in her throat, and instead, she forced herself to meet his gaze, steady and unflinching.

"Then tell me the truth, Theo," she said, her voice breaking as she stood, the movement sharp, deliberate. "Tell me what I need to know. I've seen enough to understand that my life—my father's life—wasn't built on anything real. It's all a lie. So, tell me. What am I supposed to do now?"

Theo's expression faltered for a fraction of a second, and it was enough to make Lila's pulse race. There was something in the way he looked at her now—something softer, something more vulnerable. But it was gone as quickly as it appeared, replaced by that same guarded mask he had worn from the start.

"I can't give you back what's been taken from you," he said, his voice tight. "But I can give you the choice. The choice to leave. The choice to walk away and never look back."

Lila's chest tightened, the air in the room feeling heavier with every word. She wanted to leave. She wanted to run far away from all of this—from Theo, from the man her father had been, from the life she had once known. But deep down, she knew that walking away wasn't an option. It wasn't a choice she could make. Not when everything she cared about was tangled in the web of lies that had ensnared them both.

"I don't have that luxury, do I?" she asked, her voice barely a whisper. "You've already dragged me too far into this. You've already made me part of it."

Theo stepped closer, his body now mere inches from hers. She could feel the heat radiating from him, the tension between them making her pulse quicken, her breath shallow. His eyes searched hers, as if looking for something—something he couldn't find, or perhaps something he was too afraid to ask for.

"I never wanted you to be a part of this," he repeated, his voice almost raw. "But you are. And I'll be damned if I let you get hurt."

His words hung in the air, heavy with meaning. Lila didn't know what to say, didn't know how to respond. The ache in her chest grew with every second that passed, the silence between them suffocating.

She reached up, her fingers trembling as they brushed against his cheek. It was an involuntary motion, one that felt both natural and foreign. The touch was fleeting, barely there, but it was enough to send a wave of electricity through her, to remind her of the connection they shared.

"You can't protect me from everything," she whispered. "And I don't want you to. I need to make my own choices. I need to find my own way out of this."

Theo's eyes closed for a moment, his breath uneven as he struggled to contain the storm of emotions raging inside him. When he opened his eyes again, there was a finality to his gaze that made her heart ache.

"I can't let you go," he said softly, his voice low and filled with pain. "Not now. Not after everything we've been through. Not after everything you mean to me."

Lila took a step back, the words slicing through her like a blade. Her heart pounded in her chest, a fierce storm of emotions threatening to consume her. She wanted to scream at him, to tell him how impossible everything had become, how torn she was between the truth and the man who had made her feel more alive than she had ever known. But she couldn't. She couldn't bring herself to do it.

"I don't know what to believe anymore," she said, her voice breaking. "I don't know if I can trust you. I don't know if I can trust anyone."

Theo reached for her, his hand trembling as he gently cupped her face. His thumb brushed against her skin, a soft, almost desperate motion that sent a shiver down her spine. His touch was a reminder of everything that was at stake—the love, the betrayal, the choices they had to make.

"I know," he whispered. "I know you don't trust me. But I swear to you, Lila, I never wanted to hurt you. I never wanted to drag you into this mess. But now that you're here, I can't let you go. Not without a fight."

Her breath caught in her throat, and for a moment, everything seemed to still. The storm outside, the chaos in her mind, the tension between them—it all faded into the background as she looked into his eyes.

The storm wasn't just outside.

It was inside her, too.

And there was no escaping it.

**Ten**

# The Burning Bridge

The air was thick, heavy with the weight of unspoken words. Lila stood at the edge of the balcony, looking at the city sprawling before her like an endless sea of lights and shadows. The wind tugged at her hair, but it did little to cool the fire burning inside her chest. Her thoughts were tangled, a mess of betrayal, desire, and questions she could no longer avoid. Every step she had taken had led her deeper into a world she hadn't chosen but couldn't escape. And now, standing here, on the precipice of everything she had known, she felt like she was about to fall.

She could hear the distant rumble of thunder, the storm she had felt brewing in her bones now making its presence known. It was as though the world itself had conspired to match her inner turmoil. The rain was coming, she could feel it in the air, but it was more than the storm outside that threatened to break.

It was the storm inside her—the storm she couldn't control.

Theo was standing in the doorway, watching her with a gaze that was both soft and hard, filled with the weight of everything they had been through and everything that was still to come. He had followed her in silence, waiting for her to speak first, but she couldn't find the words. Not yet.

"You're still here," she said finally, the words slipping out before she could stop them. She didn't know why she said it, but the simplicity of it seemed to say everything she was feeling. The raw vulnerability. The confusion. The longing.

Theo didn't answer immediately. His eyes were fixed on her, his gaze unwavering, as if he were trying to piece together the fractured version of her that had been revealed in the past few days. He had seen her angry, seen her terrified, but now—now he was seeing her in a way that was far more dangerous.

"Where else would I be?" he asked, his voice a quiet rumble that seemed to vibrate through the air, like the calm before a storm. "You know I can't leave. Not when everything is falling apart."

Lila turned to face him, her heart pounding in her chest. The dim light of the room flickered in his eyes, casting shadows across his face, making him look more like a stranger than the man she had once trusted. There was an ache in her chest, a gnawing emptiness that she couldn't shake. She wanted to scream at him, to demand that he explain everything—the choices he had made, the lies he had told. But most of all, she wanted to know why he hadn't told her the truth sooner.

"You should have told me," she whispered, her voice shaking despite herself. "You should have told me everything."

Theo stepped closer, his eyes narrowing slightly as he took in the anguish written on her face. "And what would that have changed, Lila?" he asked softly. "What would you have done with the truth? What would you have done with a past that's already gone? The choices we make don't change what's already been done."

She shook her head, taking a step back from him, her chest tight with frustration. "It's not about changing the past," she said, her voice thick with emotion. "It's about knowing who I'm fighting for. About knowing the people I'm supposed to trust."

Theo's expression softened, and for a brief moment, she saw the man she had once believed in, the man who had promised to protect her. But then, as quickly as it appeared, it was gone, replaced by the cold, calculating figure who had dragged her into this mess in the first place.

"You think I wanted this for you?" His voice dropped, raw and laced with pain. "You think I wanted you to know any of this? You think I wanted you to see the things I've seen, feel the things I've felt? I didn't have a choice, Lila. I didn't have a choice when I saw you standing there, looking at me with those trusting eyes."

Lila felt a flicker of something deep inside her—a mixture of guilt, confusion, and something else she couldn't quite name. "So this is my fault?" she whispered, her voice barely audible.

"No," Theo said, his voice fierce now, like a command. "This is not your fault. But it's not just mine either. We're both in this. Together. And if you think you can walk away from that, you're wrong. You can't just leave, not now. Not when they've already come for you."

The words hit her like a punch, knocking the breath from her lungs. "They?" she whispered, the terror creeping back into her veins. "Who is 'they,' Theo?"

He hesitated, and in that moment, she knew the truth was finally coming—an answer to all the questions she had buried deep inside herself, an answer she wasn't sure she was ready for.

He ran a hand through his hair, his gaze flickering toward the window as if looking for the right words. "Your father's involvement with the syndicate—it's bigger than we thought. Much bigger. There are people who are already watching you, Lila. People who are waiting for you to make a mistake. They've been waiting for you to slip."

Lila's heart stopped, and the world around her seemed to fall away. The air grew thick, and she found it hard to breathe. "What do you mean, watching me?" she whispered, her voice hoarse, the fear twisting in her chest.

"Everything you've learned, everything I've shown you—it's not just about your father anymore. It's about the power struggle that's been happening behind the scenes, and they're not going to stop until they get what they want," Theo said, his voice urgent now. He stepped closer to her, his hand brushing against hers in an almost unconscious gesture. "They'll do anything to control this, to make sure no one knows what's really been happening. They've already reached out to people inside your father's organization."

Her mind raced. It all felt like too much. Too fast. She had thought that understanding the truth would give her clarity, but it only deepened the chaos. She could feel the ground beneath her slipping away.

Theo continued, his eyes locking onto hers, filled with the weight of everything he had tried to protect her from. "They've already sent someone for you. Someone you know."

Lila's heart lurched, her breath catching in her throat. "Who?" she demanded, her voice trembling.

Theo's eyes flickered with hesitation, but he didn't look away. "Daniel," he said quietly. "He's been working for them. He's been one of the people trying to control you from the inside. Trying to keep you away from the truth."

The name hit her like a slap. Daniel—her father's most trusted associate, the man who had always been there, always known the right thing to say. The man who had promised to protect her.

"But… why?" she asked, her voice breaking. "Why would he—"

"Because he's just as tangled up in this as the rest of us," Theo interrupted, his voice hard now. "Because everyone in this game has their price. And Daniel? He made his choice long ago. He's been working for the syndicate the whole time. Trying to keep you from knowing what your father was really involved in. Trying to keep you from seeing the truth."

The world seemed to spin around her, the air growing thick with the weight of the revelation. Lila took a shaky step back, her knees almost giving way beneath her. She needed to sit down, needed to ground herself, but everything felt like it was closing in around her. She couldn't breathe. She couldn't think.

"I need to leave," she whispered, more to herself than to him. "I need to get out of here."

Theo stepped forward, his hand reaching out to steady her, but she pulled away, her chest tight with fear. "You can't leave," he said, his voice soft but filled with urgency. "You're already in too deep. And if you try to run, they'll come for you."

Lila met his gaze, and for the first time, she saw the desperation in his eyes. The desperation that mirrored her own.

There was no running now.

The bridge had burned. And she was trapped in the flames.

# Eleven

# Under the Gilded Sky

The night had settled over the city, its dark fingers creeping into every corner of her thoughts. Lila couldn't sleep. She lay in her bed, the blankets twisted around her, her heart thundering in her chest. The room was dim, lit only by the faint glow of the city's lights streaming in through the windows, casting long shadows on the floor. Her mind raced through everything that had happened—the secrets, lies, and dark revelations about her father and Daniel. But above all, she kept returning to him.

Theo.

The storm in her chest hadn't subsided. Every time she closed her eyes, she saw his face—his pain, his regret, his anger—and the look in his eyes when he had told her that leaving wasn't an option anymore. He had promised her that he would protect her, but she wasn't sure anymore if he could protect her from the world they were both caught in. The very world he had brought her into.

She turned onto her side, her eyes staring out into the empty space of the room. She had wanted to believe him. She had wanted to believe that he could be the one to save her. But now, the weight of his words lingered, like an unspoken truth that threatened to crush her.

Lila had never felt more alone.

A knock at the door broke through the silence, sharp and insistent. She stiffened, her pulse quickening as she scrambled to sit up. Her heart lurched in her chest, and for a brief moment, she thought about ignoring it. But she knew, deep down, that whoever it was wouldn't go away. Not now.

"Lila?" The voice came through the door, familiar, soft but laced with an urgency that made her blood run cold.

It was Theo.

She hesitated for a moment, her hand hovering over the door handle. Should she open it? Should she confront him now, face-to-face, after everything that had happened? The last time they had spoken, the space between them had been filled with unspoken words—words that needed to be said, but that neither of them could bring themselves to voice.

With a deep breath, she pulled open the door.

Theo stood in the doorway, his figure silhouetted by the dim light from the hallway. His jacket was unbuttoned, the collar turned up against the chill of the night air, but it wasn't the clothes that caught her attention. It was the look in his eyes— the intensity, the quiet desperation that radiated from him. His jaw was clenched, and for a moment, he didn't speak, just stood there, staring at her, as if searching for the right words.

"I didn't know where else to go," he said finally, his voice tight, filled with an emotion that made her chest tighten. "Lila, we need to talk."

Lila stepped aside, allowing him in, but the moment he crossed the threshold, the tension in the room grew heavier. The door clicked shut behind them, and they stood there, facing each other, neither of them sure of how to begin.

"Talk about what?" she asked, her voice hoarse. It was all she could manage. The walls around her heart, which had been slowly crumbling since the night she learned the truth, were now at their breaking point. She wasn't sure if she could take any more of this.

Theo seemed to wrestle with himself for a moment, his eyes flickering between hers, then the floor, then the walls as if looking for the words. But there was something in the way he stood—something she couldn't place—that made her feel like he was holding back more than just words.

"We don't have much time," he said, his voice low and strained. "They're getting closer. I know you don't want to hear it, but we have to move now, Lila. We don't have a choice."

Lila shook her head, the weight of the words sinking in like cold stone. "Move? Where? What do you mean?"

Theo stepped closer, the urgency in his eyes growing with every word. "The people who've been watching you—the ones who think they control everything—they're already making their move. They're coming for you, Lila. They're going to do whatever it takes to make sure you're theirs. And if we don't act now, if we don't leave—tonight—they'll come for you."

The reality of his words hit her like a slap, and her breath caught in her throat. Fear churned in her gut, a visceral, raw emotion that she had buried beneath anger and betrayal, and now it surged to the surface. "I don't understand," she whispered. "Why? Why me? Why now?"

Theo's gaze softened, his voice dropping even lower. "Because you're the key. You're the only person who can stop them. Your father—he was part of something bigger. A network of people who have been controlling things for years. But you… you're the last piece. You're the one who can bring it all down."

Lila stumbled back, her heart racing. The world seemed to tilt beneath her feet, spinning out of control. "What are you talking about? I don't understand. My father—he was just a businessman. He was just trying to protect us."

Theo's eyes hardened, a flash of anger crossing his features. "No, Lila. He was part of something darker than you know.

And now, they think you're the only one who can take control. You're the last heir to everything he built. The last person who can hold it all together—or destroy it."

Lila's mind spun, her pulse pounding in her ears. She had never asked for any of this. She had never wanted to be part of a world where power, greed, and manipulation were the currency. But here she was, caught between the man she thought she could trust and the man who had built an empire on lies.

"You're saying… you want me to join you?" Her voice cracked, the words tasting like ashes on her tongue. "You want me to fight for something I didn't even know existed?"

Theo took a step forward, his expression dark and intense, his eyes searching hers. "No. I don't want you to fight for anything. I want you to be free of this. But the only way to do that is to leave it behind. To leave all of it—your father, the people who think they control you, everything that's been suffocating you for so long."

For a moment, Lila didn't know what to say. The weight of his words pressed down on her like an anchor, dragging her deeper into the ocean of confusion and fear. She didn't want to be part of this war, this conspiracy. She didn't want to be the key to anything. But she couldn't deny the truth that was staring her in the face.

"I don't know if I can," she whispered. "I don't know if I can walk away from everything, Theo. From my life, from everything I've ever known."

Theo reached for her, his hands trembling as they cupped her face gently. "You don't have to walk away, Lila. You just have to choose the right side. I won't let you be part of the game. I won't let them use you."

Her breath hitched as she looked into his eyes, and for a moment, she saw something there—something real, something fragile. The love he had for her, the desperation, the pain of knowing that they were both caught in something they couldn't control.

"You think I don't know what I'm asking?" Theo's voice broke, the emotion raw and unguarded. "I don't want you to choose, Lila. I want to make it so you don't have to. But we don't have time. They're coming for you."

Her heart pounded as the storm outside seemed to grow louder, the sound of the rain mingling with the rapid beating of her chest. She could feel the weight of the world closing in around them. There was no escaping it now. She was trapped in the storm, and so was he.

"I'm not going to let them take you," Theo said, his voice fierce, filled with an intensity that left her breathless. "I'm not going to let them control you. Not when you have the power to end it."

Lila felt the tremor in her hands, the fear and the uncertainty coiling in her stomach. But beneath it all, there was something else—something she hadn't been willing to admit until now.

She wanted him. She wanted to trust him. She wanted to

believe that, together, they could break free. But the cost... the cost of it all...

"I'm with you," she said softly, the words tumbling out before she could stop them.

Theo's eyes softened, a flicker of relief in his gaze, but it was quickly replaced by determination.

"Then let's go," he whispered, pulling her into his arms.

And as the storm raged outside, Lila knew that this was it. There was no turning back now.

# Twelve

## Love's Final Stand

The streets were wet beneath their feet, slick with rain that had been falling for hours, as though the heavens themselves were trying to wash away the sins of the city. The cold air bit at Lila's skin, but it did little to quell the fire that burned inside her. The urgency of the moment—of the choice she had made—gripped her heart with a fierceness she hadn't anticipated. Every step they took together, Theo beside her, seemed like both a leap forward and a step into the unknown.

Lila kept her eyes fixed straight ahead, her pulse quickening with every passing second. The shadows seemed to stretch longer in the rain-soaked streets, and the city had never felt more alive—more dangerous—than it did now. It was a place where nothing and no one were what they seemed, and she had learned that truth the hard way.

Her fingers brushed against Theo's, and she felt the familiar spark of warmth between them. It was a fragile thing, fleeting and full of tension, like the calm before a storm. She wanted to believe in it, to believe that they could escape this madness together. But she couldn't ignore the cold reality that surrounded them—the danger that had followed them from the shadows.

"They'll be after us soon," Theo said, his voice low and filled with a quiet urgency. He was right beside her, his presence a constant, grounding force in the chaos that had consumed her life. "We need to move faster. We need to stay ahead of them."

Lila didn't reply at first, her mind racing with the weight of his words. She could feel the tension building between them, the unspoken acknowledgment that this was it—this was the point of no return. There would be no turning back from this, no escaping the choices they had made.

She glanced up at him, her heart aching with the desire to believe in his promise. "Theo," she said, her voice barely a whisper, "are you sure this is the right thing? I don't know if I can trust anyone anymore. I don't know who I'm supposed to be."

Theo turned to her, his eyes dark and unreadable in the dim light, but there was a flicker of something softer there, something that made her chest tighten. His hand moved, almost instinctively, to cup her face, his thumb brushing gently over her skin.

"You've always known who you are, Lila," he said quietly.

"You've just been too afraid to see it. But we're in this together now. And no matter what happens, we face it together. You and me."

His words, filled with sincerity and pain, settled over her like a blanket, soothing the fear that gnawed at her insides. She wanted to believe him. She wanted to believe that, together, they could fight against everything that had been done to them.

But there was something else, something lingering at the edges of her mind—the haunting realization that they might be too late. That the world they were about to enter would swallow them whole.

Before she could respond, the sound of a car engine cut through the night, low and menacing, and her breath caught in her throat. Theo's grip on her tightened, his eyes scanning the street. He didn't need to say a word. They both knew. The danger had found them.

"Run," Theo said, his voice sharp, filled with a raw urgency.

Without thinking, Lila turned, her heart pounding in her chest, and ran. Her legs burned with every step, the sound of her heels clicking against the wet pavement echoing in the night. She could hear Theo's footsteps behind her, matching hers in the rhythm of desperation. They ran in silence, the sound of their breath heavy in the night, the world around them blurring as they raced toward an uncertain future.

She didn't know where they were going. She didn't care. The

only thing that mattered was staying ahead of whatever—or whoever—was coming for them.

The city seemed to close in around her as they turned a corner, the buildings looming like giants in the dark, their windows dark and lifeless. The rain had started to come down harder now, drenching them both, but Lila barely noticed. All she could feel was the frantic beat of her heart, the terror rising in her throat as she ran.

Theo was beside her, his face a mask of determination, but she could see the strain in his eyes. He wasn't just running from the danger behind them; he was running from the future they both knew might not come. She wanted to scream, to ask him what they were fighting for. But she already knew the answer. They were fighting for each other. Fighting for a chance at something that had never been possible before.

They rounded another corner, and the sound of the car engine grew louder, closer. Lila's chest tightened, her breath coming in short gasps, but she didn't slow down. She couldn't. The darkness behind them was closing in, and the only thing that mattered was keeping ahead of it.

Suddenly, Theo's hand shot out, grabbing her wrist and pulling her into an alleyway. She stumbled, almost losing her balance, but he steadied her, his grip firm and unwavering.

"Stay quiet," he whispered urgently. His voice was tight with tension, his face pale from the effort of their escape. "They're too close. We need to hide."

Lila nodded, her body trembling with a mix of fear and adrenaline. The alley was narrow, the walls towering above them like silent sentinels. The air was thick with the scent of wet concrete and something darker, something that made her skin crawl. But she didn't care. Not now. Not when everything was on the line.

They pressed themselves into the shadows, the wetness of the brick walls seeping into her clothes as she crouched down beside Theo. Her pulse raced, and she could hear her breath, shallow and erratic, in the silence of the alley. Every second felt like an eternity, every movement filled with the possibility of being caught.

Theo's hand brushed against hers again, his fingers wrapping around hers in a tight grip. She looked at him, her breath catching in her throat as their gazes locked. There was so much left unsaid between them—so much that neither of them was ready to admit—but in that moment, she knew that this was it. The moment when everything would either fall apart or be rebuilt from the ashes.

"I'll protect you," Theo whispered, his voice barely audible. "I promise."

Lila's chest ached as she stared at him, her heart torn between the desire to trust him completely and the fear that he was only leading her further into a trap. But the truth was, she couldn't walk away now. She had already stepped too far into this world. And no matter what happened next, she would face it with him.

A sudden flash of headlights illuminated the alley, cutting through the darkness like a blade. The car had found them.

Lila's breath caught in her throat, and Theo's grip on her tightened as he pulled her further into the shadows, his body a shield between her and the oncoming danger. The car slowed, its engine purring like a predator, and Lila could hear the soft crunch of tires on wet pavement as it came to a stop just a few feet away.

Her heart pounded in her chest, the sound deafening in her ears. She could feel the heat of Theo's body against hers, the tension in his muscles, as they waited in the darkness, frozen, holding their breath.

The door of the car opened, and a figure stepped out into the rain. Lila couldn't make out their face in the dim light, but the silhouette was enough. She could feel the danger radiating from them, like an electric charge in the air.

Theo's hand tightened around hers, and he whispered, "Stay quiet. We can't let them find us."

The figure paused, looking around the alley, and Lila held her breath. Her heart hammered in her chest as the seconds ticked by. Every instinct in her screamed at her to move, to run, but she stayed frozen, her body pressed against the cold brick wall, every muscle tensed with fear.

Then, the figure turned and began walking toward the alley, their steps slow, deliberate. They were getting closer.

Lila's mind raced, the adrenaline flooding her veins as she realized that this was it. This was their last chance.

She turned to Theo, her voice barely a whisper. "We have to move now."

Theo's eyes flickered with determination, and in that moment, she saw it—the man she had known all along. He was going to fight for them. For her.

He nodded, his lips curling into a grim smile. "On three. One… two… three."

And with that, they moved.